Get the best from a career break

How to make the most of your time away from the office

A BLOOMSBURY REFERENCE BOOK
Created from the Bloomsbury Business Database
www.ultimatebusinessresource.com

© Bloomsbury Publishing Plc 2005

First published in 2005 by
Bloomsbury Publishing Plc
38 Soho Square
London W1D 3HB

British Library Cataloguing in Publication Data
A CIP record for this book is available from the British Library.

ISBN 0–7475–7739–0

Design by Fiona Pike, Pike Design, Winchester
Typeset by RefineCatch Limited, Bungay, Suffolk
Printed in Italy by Legoprint

All papers used by Bloomsbury Publishing are natural, recyclable
products made from wood grown in well-managed forests. The
manufacturing processes conform to the environmental regulations
of the country of origin.

Contents

How can *you* make the most of a career break?

For each of the questions below, choose whichever answer best suits you, work out your score, then read the guidelines to find out how you can to get the best from a career break.

What is your main concern about career break?
a) Making it work.
b) What to do during it.
c) Whether to take one at all.

How determined are you to have a career break?
a) 100% – nothing will stop me.
b) It's an ambition but I'm worried about my job security and finances.
c) It's an option but I'm not sure it's the right choice for me.

How would you describe your current plans?
a) Realistic and thorough.
b) Exciting, but I'm not sure if they will work.
c) Non-existent. I'll wing it.

What are you priorities?
a) Fulfilling my ambitions.

b) Enjoying life and spending time with friends and family.
c) My career.

Who have you discussed your plans with?
a) My boss, friends, and family.
b) My friends and family.
c) No-one.

What will you do if your request is turned down?
a) I've researched and identified several back-up plans.
b) I've begun thinking of other ways to break the work routine.
c) I don't have a Plan B yet.

What worries do you have about life after your break?
a) Whether to change jobs.
b) Returning to my old job.
c) Whether my career will have been affected in the long term.

How would you describe your career break objectives?
a) Very clear.
b) Slowly taking shape.
c) Uncertain.

Which of the following best describes your thoughts about taking time out?
a) I've worked out which path would suit my needs.
b) I know the options open to me but can't pick one.
c) I've not thought about the different options yet.

a = **1**, **b** = **2**, and **c** = **3**.

Now add up your scores.

Everyone should read Chapter **1**, as it will help you to balance the pros of a career break against the cons, and reminds you of alternative options.

- **9–14:** You've clearly been considering this for a while, and have probably gone through the preliminary planning stages. Read Chapter **4** for help with sorting out your finances. It is also well worth thinking about life after your break. Chapter **6** considers the shorter term, while Chapter **7** will help you to look further forward.

- **15–21:** You're nearly there! Chapter **2** will guide you through working out your priorities, so you can best plan your next step. As well as helping to clarify your plans, this will be extremely useful when you come to putting your plans to your boss (if you haven't already done so). Do make sure you have considered all the alternatives by reading Chapters **3** and **5**.

- **22–27:** You need to be aware of what a large change in your life a career break will make. To help you to consider whether it really is for you, work out your priorities with the help of Chapter **2**. Maybe another option might be better at this stage in your career – see Chapter **3** for more on this.

Weighing up the pros and cons of a career break

A career break is some time away from your usual working role and everyday routine. There are many positive reasons to consider taking one: starting a family is the most common one, but study, travel, trying out a business idea, or caring for family members are other positive priorities that set people thinking along these lines.

People may also take a break to get away from *negative* aspects of their career, though. Stress and pressure, office politics, and turbulent periods of upheaval can all make employees look for a change of scene. This allows them to recharge their batteries, get back in touch with their core values, and maintain their health.

If you do take a career break, you have some options to think about once you get back; you might return to your old job or look for a new challenge when you're ready. These days companies are more likely to look favourably on career breaks and some companies have flexible, enlightened polices that go well beyond what they're compelled to do by law. Rather than lose the investment already made in your training and development, they agree to career breaks in the hope that their people will eventually return to

employment with increased commitment, renewed loyalty, a broader perspective, and new skills.

Step one: Think through your concerns

1 I've been working for quite a while now. Am I throwing away everything I've achieved if I take a break?

While time off doing *nothing* will be very hard to sell on your CV, having and achieving some valuable personal objectives during your time away may well affect your career for the better. You'll often be perceived with respect (and perhaps a little jealousy) for having the initiative, confidence, and determination to realise a dream. You'll need to make sure that you communicate what you've gained from your break clearly and positively, though. Stress the benefits when you describe what you've been doing and quantify your achievements if you can. For example, if you have management skills and you have been working overseas for a charity, you could say: 'I helped secure finance for a health centre which enabled it to take on three more members of staff and increase its impact in the community.'

2 What are the main obstacles?

Your other priorities are actually the main obstacles. The most common reasons for not taking a long career break are to do with one's partner, family, career, house, career, or sporting ambitions. For most people, giving up work for a period of time means a loss of income on which they have become dependent. This can seem like a scary prospect.

In general, the younger you are and the less routine your life is, the less inhibited you may feel about taking the plunge. At the other end of the spectrum, there are some lucky people for whom a career break of 12 or 24 months can be managed on savings alone, allowing them to return to pick up their previous routine without any material change.

3 Will my skills start to look 'tired'?

12 months away from a role will not generally leave you with a skills issue. The more technical your role and the longer you spend away from it, though, the more time and effort you will have to put into staying in touch and keeping up to speed.

Some employers, for example in healthcare professions, find it so important to retain good workers that they'll not only allow them to take a lengthy break, but also fund their skills updates on their return. In other areas, it may be down to you to get yourself back up to speed. For more specific advice on this area, talk to the relevant managers in your company or organisation or contact an industry body for advice. If you belong to a trade union, they may also be able to help.

4 Can I be made redundant while on my career break?

Unfortunately, yes. Your employer is expected to consult with you and your trade union in the usual way. If your employer decides to select you for redundancy *solely* because you are on a career break, though, this could be held to be unfair redundancy selection.

The length of time you've been working for your employer will have a bearing on the situation. If you have 12 months' continuous service, you are protected against unfair dismissal, including unfair selection for redundancy, and if you have two years' continuous service, you are also entitled to a redundancy payment.

A break of one week will break this continuity, except under circumstances where it is customary for such absence to count for continuity. If, therefore, you can show that absence on a career break constitutes such circumstances, you'd be protected. As this is a complex area, discuss it with your employer and ask for a statement about continuity to be added to any letters regarding your career break arrangements.

Step two: Decide on your objectives

Step back and take some time to ask yourself why a career break holds such appeal. You need to start off with an idea of what you hope to experience or achieve. What secondary or underlying objectives do you have? Chapter 2 will help you look at your values and priorities in life in more depth.

✔ Visualise the beginning, middle, and end of your time away and your eventual return to work. Make notes about how you want it to be in an *ideal* situation, but also think about how it might work realistically.

TOP TIP

Being clear about what you want to get out of your time away is really important. Thinking about your break in detail needn't dampen your spirit of adventure; in fact, it will probably help it along, as the more you investigate how things might work in reality, the more likely it is that you'll follow through and make a success of your break.

Step three: Talk it through with those closest to you

Remember that people other than yourself may be affected by your decision to have a career break—this is especially the case if you have dependants.

✔ Make sure that you talk to the important people in your life about your plans and that you have their backing before you take your ideas any further. You can, of course, decide to ignore their advice if they're not pleased about it, but it's worth asking yourself whether your relationship with that person (or those people) is more important to you than your planned break. Is there a compromise situation that would work well for everyone concerned?

Step four: Talk to your boss about it

If you've decided to take your idea further, the next person to talk to is your boss.

✔ Be clear in your mind about everything you want when you broach the subject with him or her. Take along some notes as prompts if you'd find that helpful.

✔ Know what you are asking for, including the length of time away, pay and benefits, continuity of employment, possibility of return to the same role, and so on. To make the idea seem as attractive as possible, you need to be able to explain what benefits your break will bring both for you and your employer, and prepare a statement about wanting to return.

✔ Make a business case that would encourage your employer to support your request. For example, let's say that you work for a large multinational organisation but that you'd like to spend some time abroad learning Spanish. You could say that the language skills you'd gain on your break would be put to good use when you return, as you'd be able to liaise more quickly and effectively with your organisation's branches in both Europe and Latin America.

✔ You could also find out whether there's a policy that provides for sponsored sabbaticals. Your employer might be prepared to provide what you request, or suggest a compromise.

TOP TIP

Be ready to be flexible and to meet your employer half-way. Remember that your request may have come completely out of the blue, so he or she may feel a bit 'ambushed'. Depending on your relationship with your boss, you might want to e-mail him or her about your idea first, just to give a broad-strokes outline that you can then discuss in more detail—this may lessen the shock-value somewhat when you come to talk face-to-face.

Step five: Be ready in case the answer's 'no'

You have to be prepared for things not going to plan. If your request is turned down, keep calm and try to find out the reasons behind the decision. The provision of career breaks is purely at the discretion of your employer, but if they are made available only to women, then the powers-that-be are clearly behaving in a discriminatory manner.

If other work colleagues have been granted similar time off for parental or study purposes and you have not been supplied with a satisfactory explanation as to why you have not, you may want to claim a grievance through your personnel department (if your company has one) or your union.

Even though you're bound to feel disappointed at first, look at the positive aspect of your company's decision: freedom. If you're *that* committed to the idea of the career break, you'll just go anyway, even if your employer won't keep your job open. The obvious downside to your employer of agreeing to a break is that you are obligated to return. You may feel very differently about the prospect of going back to your old job once you've been away for a while, so in a way you've been relieved of that decision.

Step six: Think about other ways of achieving your goals

There are a variety of back-up plans available to you if your career break request does get turned down. Whether they suit you will depend largely on what you're planning to do on your career break, but you could consider:

1 **Part-time work.** This can free you up to realise your dreams without having to take such a significant drop in earnings. If you stay with the same employer, it can also give you continuity of routine and of your social network, both of which can help to reduce the stress related to big changes in your life.

2 **Working from home, sometimes called 'teleworking'.** This option can allow you more time in your chosen environment and it may also give you the flexibility to control when you work. Many people choose this option since it gives them fewer financial headaches than reducing their hours, and it's particularly convenient for people with new or growing families. There is a negative side to it, unfortunately, in that even if you do go down this route, work will still eat up reasonably large chunks of your time and attention and you may feel isolated outside of your everyday comfort zone. It may also mean that you can't spend as much time focusing on the new challenges you're hoping to explore. It's worth spending some time thinking through an average working week and seeing how that might translate to a home-office setting.

3 **Working abroad.** This can be a great way to satisfy a craving for novelty and variety while furthering your career ambitions at the same time. It is the best way to master a foreign language and to gain an understanding of a nation's culture, as you are totally immersed in it. Don't forget the financial benefits too: you'll still be earning something, so this is a good way to fund your itchy feet.

You may choose to work within your usual field through a secondment or a change of employer, or you may go for a complete change, such as picking grapes or teaching English.

TOP TIP

If you are an EU citizen, working within other member countries is relatively easy but remember that if you want to go further afield, you'll have to apply for work permits/visas, some of which can be tricky to get hold of. Whatever you do, make sure you have all the necessary documents before you travel to your chosen destination.

---

4 **Changing employer.** Looking for a new job can give you the chance to negotiate terms as part of your contract, with a view to a future break. This works for study breaks and for travel abroad but may not be suitable for parental breaks, the timescale for which may already be dictated! If you (or your partner) are already expecting a baby, changing employer could result in a loss of rights to parental leave. For example, while all pregnant employees have a right to 26 weeks' ordinary maternity leave, you can only take additional maternity leave (an extra 26 weeks' unpaid leave) if you have 26 weeks' continuous service with your employer at the 14th week of your pregnancy. This may not affect you right at the moment, but it's worth bearing in mind. The

DTI website is a great source of help here, and you'll find the address at the end of the chapter.

TOP TIP

Looking for a new role on return can give you complete freedom, and it's certainly a good option if you're hoping to take an extended career break. It may also be the most suitable route if you intend to retrain, take a completely new direction in your career, or care for children or other family members in the long term.

Step seven: Take the plunge!

✔ Look back over the notes you took when you were daydreaming about your career break and prioritise your objectives. Which are most important to you? These are the 'core' of what you will achieve. Think about the obstacles that may stand in your way and the contingency plans you'll need to make to deal with them. Obviously you can't see all the potential events that may throw you off course, but attempting to identify the most obvious will bring your plan into the real world.

✔ Identify the gap between where you are now and where you want to be. Start breaking it up into manageable 'chunks' and then identify milestones along the way. For example, if you are planning a trip abroad, your first chunk is research about your destination(s), and the first milestone is knowing which visas and work permits are required.

TOP TIP

Having a plan will help you move efficiently towards your goals, but don't feel you have to stick to it rigidly. You may decide to rethink your objectives as a result of experiences you have early on, so try to remain focused but be flexible too. Once you get used to planning in the way outlined above, you'll find you waste less time worrying or dithering.

Step eight: Tie up loose ends

If you decide to leave your current job when you go on your career break, make sure that you leave with the best possible reputation so that you'll get a glowing reference. This also leaves you with the option of being able to apply to your previous employer for work when you get back, if you'd like to.

If you *are* planning to return to the same role it after your break, it's even more important to make sure that tasks are properly completed or handed over efficiently, and that you train your successor as well as possible. Start making a list of important contacts and duties well in advance of your leaving date to act as a helpful resource to others in your absence. If at all possible, set up a hand-over period so that your successor can see what you do on an everyday basis.

Common mistakes

✗ You don't keep in touch

Keeping in touch is vitally important if you want a smooth transition back into your previous role. It's also important if you will be moving on to a new career. Keep up with who's who and catch up with relevant communications in your business or industry. The Internet has made this much easier to do these days, wherever you are, but company publications or trade journals might be a big help too. If you feel it's right for you, and you are taking some time out to complete a course of study, you could spend your holiday time back at work.

✗ You feel trapped by finances

Working out financial matters can be difficult, but it can be done as long as you're clear about your priorities. For example, identify where your money currently goes. What could you achieve with a different plan? Weigh up the benefits of continuing as you are, compared to spending on your career break. Are there ways to reduce spending so that you can save for a career break in advance? To release yourself from feeling 'trapped', remind yourself of your priorities and choices. Turn to Chapter 2 for more detailed advice on this key issue.

STEPS TO SUCCESS

✔ If you've been thinking about taking a career break, be clear about what you'd like to achieve and the ways in which it would benefit you.

✔ Be honest with yourself and others about your plans and discuss your thoughts with those closest to you before you talk to your boss: things will be a lot easier if you have the support of your friends and family.

✔ Think through the practicalities of your plans in as much detail as you can. This shouldn't dampen your enthusiasm for your big adventure, but will make you better equipped to actually make it happen and spot potential problem areas now, so that you can work out ways round them.

✔ If you broach the idea with your boss, you might want to send him or her an e-mail about it first, so that your face-to-face meeting isn't coloured by your news coming as a bolt from the blue.

✔ In your conversation, stress to your boss how the business might actually benefit from your time away: you may gain new skills that would be useful when you're back.

✔ Be flexible and be prepared to compromise in some areas if your boss can't agree to every single one of your requests. You're embarking on a negotiation, remember, and successful ones work out well when both sides are ready to give and take.

✔ If your request is completely dismissed, you have some options. Again, their appeal to you will depend on what you want to do with your time away, but you could think about working part-time, from home, or abroad. If the worst comes to the worst, you could look for a new job and negotiate a career break as part of your new package.

✔ Whether you're leaving your present job for good or returning to it after your career break, tie up all loose ends and help your successor settle in well. If you're leaving, a good reputation will help you get an excellent reference; if you're going to come back, you'll know you haven't left an awful mess for someone else to sort out.

Useful links

Career Breaker.com:
www.careerbreaker.com
DTI Employment Relations—Regulatory Advice (Maternity):
www.dti.gov.uk/er/maternity.htm
Handbag.com:
www.handbag.com/careers/careerbreak/studyleave
Raising Kids—Family Finance:
www.raisingkids.co.uk/fi/fi_03.asp

Teaching English as a foreign language (TEFL) — Training:

www.tefltraining.co.uk

TEFL chat and information pages:

www.tefl.net

Worldwide TEFL jobs database:

www.tefl.com

VSO:

www.vso.org.uk

Thinking about the 'bigger' picture: values and priorities

If you're thinking about taking a career break, you're probably thinking about the 'bigger' picture of the rest of your life too. A yearning to have a break from work can be just that—a wish to escape the same old, same old—but it may also be a symptom of your work–life balance being out of kilter and a sign that you need to rethink your priorities.

This chapter will help you think about what you value in life. Sounds obvious? Not really. When was the last time you really thought about it? Think about how much your life might have changed over the past five years, say. Do you have new commitments, or have you suffered any losses that mean that you think differently about things?

Whether you decide to take a career break or not, re-examining what you value may be something that's well overdue. It will certainly help improve your work–life balance before or after your break. The steps below will help you to break down what the factors are in your current work–life balance and to organise yourself according to their relative importance to you. Remember that what is right for you will change, so make

time to check it regularly and adjust it as you need to.

Step one: Work out what's important to you

Divide up a page into the following areas:

- Me
- Partner/Family
- Work/Career
- Finances
- Friends/Hobbies/Leisure
- Health

Write down the things that you feel passionately about in each of these areas. You may find that there are a lot of overlaps, and you may also find that some boxes have lots in while others have very little. Don't worry about this—there are no hard and fast rules.

| Real life example |

Me	Earn respect. Be loving. Don't hurt others. Space and downtime for me. Learning and growing. Time to sit and think. Recharge batteries.
Partner/Family	Love. Two-way support. Time together. Teamwork. Atmosphere.

Work/Career	Earning. Integrity. Professionalism. Collegiate atmosphere. Challenges. Lots of interaction with people. Building something for the future. Being respected. Having a good reputation.
Finances	Earning enough to be comfortable. Planning ahead. Investing wisely where possible.
Friends/Hobbies/ Leisure	Lots of interaction with people. Holidays with others.
Health	Fitness. Good physical appearance. Good mental health.

If you find this difficult to do, here's another way of getting at your values.

✔ Close your eyes, imagine yourself at a much older age, looking back at your life. First, imagine that you've had a really full and satisfying life. Take a sheet of paper and write down the things that you're proud to have done. What were the best bits that give you joy to remember? Now imagine that you're looking back over a wasted life. What do you regret and what do you wish you had done more of?

2 Real life example 2

Time and energy well spent in a full and satisfying life:

■ My family: time spent talking, communicating with

them, helping them develop, just being together, loving and being loved.

- Building solid friendships for love, sharing, support, and learning.
- My business: created something bigger than myself, developed great understanding of clients' needs, developed new ways to help.
- Helping others.
- Developing myself to understand others better.

In a wasted life I would regret:
- Not travelling and learning about other cultures.
- Wasting time on appearances rather than substance.
- Lost contacts with family and friends.
- Staying employed all my life for the 'security'.
- Wasting my creativity.
- Harming others or failing to help where help was needed and I was able.
- Poor health as a result of not looking after my body.

Step two: Translate these thoughts into a single list of your values

✔ Write, in a couple of words, the essence of each of the thoughts you've listed in the previous exercises, with no repeats. Sometimes two or three of your original thoughts might be summarised under a single heading.

TOP TIP

Values are very personal and so are the definitions that we use. Don't worry too much about the words that you use here; other people may interpret them differently, but that doesn't matter. The important thing is that *you* know what you mean by a particular label.

For example, the labels you could use are:

- Love and fun
- Respect
- Harnessing thought and creativity
- Development and support (self and others)
- Communication and interaction
- Earning/being productive
- Holping others
- Building for a better future

Step three: Work out the relative importance of these values to you

Values tend to be hierarchical, which means that you can prioritise them. As the next step in the process, rank your values in order of their importance to you.

TOP TIP

For you to get the best out of the exercise,
don't allow any values to 'tie' (that is,
be joint first, joint second, and so on);
the list has to be a real rank in
order of importance. It may take
you a while to get the order right
for you, but don't give up too soon.

For example:

1 Love and fun
2 Respect
3 Building for a better future
4 Helping others
5 Earning/being productive
6 Development and support (self and others)
7 Communication and interaction
8 Harnessing thought and creativity

✔ To check that the order you've chosen is right for you,
  ask yourself: 'If I have value no. 1 (in this case, love and
  fun) in my life, will I have value no. 2 (respect)?' And so on
  down the hierarchy.

✔ If the answer is 'yes', then they're in the right order for
  you. If the answer is 'no', try a different order, until each
  pair feels right.

TOP TIP
It may seem that logically your values might not be linked in this way, but try to suspend your logic while you try the step above.
Values are internal and sometimes irrational, but there is a 'natural' order to them. Clarifying the hierarchy of your values is a very powerful step in helping you to prioritise in a way that is more satisfactory _for you_.

✔ The second check is to start at the bottom of the hierarchy and ask: 'Does value 8 (harnessing thought and creativity) support and contribute to value 7 (communication and interaction)?'

Because the relationships between the values are based on _your_ beliefs about living, others may not find them strictly logical or make any sense of them. As long as they make sense to you, though, you'll derive benefit from them. Remember that your beliefs are built up from a very young age as you learn from your experiences. As you work through this exercise, you may experience moments of insight about why certain elements of your life balance are the way they are. For example, if you shared the values displayed in the examples above, you may find that your great drive to 'build a better future' is fuelled by the belief that this will contribute to 'respect' and therefore allow you to 'be loved and have fun'.

Step four: Set yourself some goals

Now you need to bring the results of the exercises into the real world and translate them into positive action.

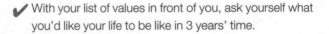 With your list of values in front of you, ask yourself what you'd like your life to be like in 3 years' time.

✔ Write your answer in the positive present tense, making sure that your answer is as fully descriptive and as positive as you can be.

You may end up with three or four bullet points for each value. Some of these may be statements about things that you regularly do, others may be specific qualifications achieved or goals met. Include how you'll feel about your achievements.

For example:

Value: love and fun
The family eats together most evenings and we chat about our day and our plans. We set aside time for homework and encourage the children through our example, sitting down with them where possible. At weekends I spend plenty of time playing with the children and finding new ideas or environments to introduce to them. We also allow them time without direct supervision. My partner and I make time to relax together and just

be in each other's company, whether with friends or alone.

or

Value: interest
I go for lots of walks with no pressure of time at weekends, and enjoy the house and local countryside. I feel really fit and in tune with the seasons. I can consider investment projects and get through the reading I want to do. I spend lots of time on creative things, such as painting, music, and socialising.

When you read back through your 3-year plan, it should feel inspiring. When you read it, it should make you feel, 'Yes, this is what I am working towards'. If it doesn't, go back through your values and see which is not fully implemented in your plan.

✔ Once you're happy with the 3-year statements do the same for 1 year's time. Bear in mind that three 1-year plans must add up to the 3-year plan.

✔ Next, plan for 6 months' time, again in the positive present tense. Remember to make this realistic and in tune with the 1-year plan.

✔ Finally write your 1-month plan. You could turn some elements of this plan into a diary, if you find that helpful.

Make sure that you're as positive, clear and descriptive as you can be about what you've achieved by the end of the month. Be careful about the goals you set, though, and plan in advance how much progress is 'enough'. There are only 24 hours in a day and you may not be able to fit everything in. Remember to give yourself a break even as you work towards achieving your goals. If you don't think your plan is realistic, think back over the long term. Ask yourself:

- which opportunities are only available now?
- which things can take a back seat for the moment without negatively affecting my life balance?

TOP TIP

The 3–1–6–1 plan is very powerful and can act as a fantastic motivational tool too. As you work through the steps, you'll become very clear about, and very active in, the choices you're making and this will help you feel more in control of your destiny and your balance. When you feel your motivation dipping or your balance slipping, refer back to your plan and review the choices you've made. Are they still right for you or should something change? Remember that the plan's not set in stone; it just a way of laying out what you're hoping and working for. Make it flexible so that when *you* change (as we all do), your plan will also change. Review the plan each month and then write the next month's.

Common mistakes

✗ **You confuse other people's values for your own**

When we're young we learn a lot from our parents, siblings, teachers, and other people with prominent roles in our lives. We also take on others' values. Later, as we become more independent, we may test and throw out some of what we've learnt and we go through a transition period during which our adult 'persona' is formed. Adults often carry with them the 'voices' of important others, reminding them of 'musts', 'shoulds', and 'oughts' and sometimes people find these useful.

Be aware of these voices as you go through the steps in this section. Do you *really* agree with them deep down? Are still they helpful to you? Or have the 'oughts' and 'shoulds' become tyrannical, pushing you to do things that aren't resonant with your values? Watch out for times when you use these words and ask yourself if they're coming from within you or from others. Are they right for you?

✗ **You don't take into account other people's needs**

Although the process outlined above focuses mainly on you and how you think and feel about things, do check in regularly with the important people in your life as you work through it. Perhaps they'll want to think about their values too, so that you can see which are truly compatible and where important differences lie. Don't see this as a threat to your relationship with them, but rather as a way to help you to appreciate each other's positions better in the future. Your plan may very well require support or direct input from these people, so it will be important to see whether your plan takes their needs and timings into account. For example, if you have a family, the plan has a much better chance of working if you're all on the same wavelength than if you're all planning in different directions.

STEPS TO SUCCESS

✔ Values are the motivational elements that drive our actions and reactions. They're built up throughout our lives and have been shown to work hierarchically. Knowing the relative importance of your values can give you great insight into why you act and react the way you do.

✔ Create a plan that includes the elements you need to have in balance. Setting goals around these elements draws you toward the future you would like.

✔ Others have an effect on our values and on our plans. Don't forget to talk to those who share your life.

Useful links

Life-balance Newsletter by e-mail:
www.coachange.co.uk/cgi-bin/page.pl?p=balance
Understand your priorities:
**http://www.mindtools.com/pages/article/
newHTE_02.htm**

Think about the options open to you

As with most things in life, the secret of a successful career break is careful planning. While some career breaks are dictated by circumstance—such as parenthood, illness, or redundancy for example—it is remarkable how few breaks are properly prepared for.

According to a survey by the Institute of Physics, the majority of their members on career breaks made minimal or no plans for what they were going to do with their time away from work, and felt isolated and dissatisfied as a result! On the other hand, spent wisely, a career break can actually enhance your career prospects and give you a whole new outlook on life.

To make the most of a wonderful opportunity, then, it's important to think through your options carefully and decide what will best suit you and your circumstances. Are you looking for a short break as part of your annual leave, a slightly longer break that doesn't require too much effort to persuade the boss, or the longer, life-altering experience? This chapter explores the main choices available.

Step one: Decide whether your aim is to learn something new

A career break is often the ideal chance to immerse yourself in learning something different—whether it's to advance your professional skills or to pursue an old or new interest. There are a number of ways you can approach this, from gaining your employer's blessing for a short break away from your job, to quitting altogether and embarking on complete retraining for a new career. The main options are as follows:

1 **Paid sabbaticals.** A paid sabbatical is when your employer gives you leave of absence, often on full pay, to gain knowledge that will boost your skills and prospects within your current job. This learning may be paid for either by you or by your employer. For example, if you are in a management position, your company might well feel that it would be a good idea for you to do an MBA (Master of Business Administration degree), and fund the training. Many organisations—particularly large employers like the health service—use sabbaticals as reward schemes for long service, or in order to retain valuable staff.

2 **Unpaid study leave.** Study leave is time off work to embark on an educational course that's not necessarily related to your job. Your employer agrees to make your job—or a similar one—available to you at the end of the study leave, and you agree to return to work on a specific date. If you've always longed to join an archaeological dig

or pursue your passion for fine art, taking a career break of this kind could be a way of making your dream come true. The downside is that pay and benefits usually stop, and you may temporarily cease to be an employee of your company. Such breaks typically last anything from one to five years.

3 **Retraining.** If you've decided to swap your current career for a different one you may need to leave your job altogether while you gain the new skills or qualifications you need. There are a bewildering number of courses and training providers in the marketplace, so it's important to think about you what you want carefully before you choose one. Decide what you'd like your future role to be; identify the skills and qualifications you'll need, and then work out where the gaps are. Think about:

- personal skills—communication, teamwork, managing time
- technical skills—for example, using computer applications, catering, retail, horticulture
- qualifications—A-levels, degrees, NVQs, HNCs, etc
- finances—how expensive the training is, and how you'll manage for money while studying
- time available

You then also need to think about what format of training will be most suitable for you and your personal circumstances. For example, would you prefer a full- or part-time course in a college or university, a distance-learning programme that you can undertake at your own pace, or a one-off event on a specific topic? The government sponsored Learndirect website (see the end of the chapter) can be a helpful starting point when looking for a suitable course.

Negotiating with your employer

Many employers are likely to be agreeable to the idea of sabbaticals or study leave, and may have formal career-break schemes in place. Schemes like these are a good way of demonstrating long-term commitment to employees, and organisations also benefit from the fact that people who return from extended leave are more likely to want to stay in their current job rather than move on to another. Study breaks are also easy and cheap to organise and help to prevent mid-career burnout.

If your employer has a career-break policy:

- check if you're eligible for it
- look at the terms of the break, such as pension benefits, arrangements for keeping in touch, and returning to work. Do these meet your requirements?

If not:

- find out what other similar organisations are offering
- collect information to sell the idea to your managers
- ask your professional organisation or union to help you in your negotiations

Put your case in writing and stress the benefits of study leave to the organisation. If you're successful, it's essential to ask for a formal agreement with your employer. You then both know where you stand and have something to refer to in any future discussions.

TOP TIP

One downside to keep in mind when considering a career break is that it can be very difficult to get back into work afterwards, especially if you're returning to the same job as before. This is particularly true when you have used your break to do something completely 'off topic'—you may find that you are not the same person as you were before, and that your job no longer suits who you are! Turn to Chapter 7 for advice on looking for a new challenge.

Step two: Think about a secondment

If you enjoy what you do but feel as if you need some 'fresh air', think about taking a temporary secondment. This might be a good choice, as employers are increasingly recognising that secondment can be valuable for development. Over recent years, organisations have adopted flatter management structures (that is, there are fewer levels in the hierarchy) and opportunities for promotion aren't easy to come by. Secondment offers an alternative way of keeping employees fresh and developing their skills.

1 Types of secondment
Secondments usually take one of two forms:

- **Internal**, to another department within the same organisation, which is a particularly useful way of resourcing short-term assignments or projects. The *advantage* is that you gain wider experience and new skills without the disruption of relocation and with the benefit of continuity of employment; the *disadvantage* is that you don't get the completely fresh outlook that an external secondment may bring.
- **External**, to another organisation (public sector to private or vice versa, for example, or to a voluntary organisation). The *advantage* is that you can gain experience of a completely different working environment, industry, or professional discipline; the *disadvantages* are that you may experience culture shock in your new organisation, or find it difficult to settle back into your old one when you return after the secondment.

2 Duration and payment
The duration of a secondment depends on circumstances. Short-term deployments may last less than 100 hours (often part time); long-term ones can be for a year or more.

Generally speaking, your employer will continue to pay your salary during the secondment period, though if you're being 'lent out' on a commercial basis, the costs may well be paid back by the organisation you're seconded to.

3 Eligibility and recruitment

Eligibility for secondment usually varies from organisation to organisation. It may be open to all, or have restrictions such as only being offered to managers, technical and professional staff, high fliers, or employees with a specified length of service. Recruitment methods also vary, but generally speaking the process should be no different to that for a normal job—advertisement, application, interview, and so on.

4 Success factors

For a secondment to be successful, everyone concerned— you, your regular employer, and your temporary employer— needs to be clear about their expectations, accountabilities, responsibilities, and objectives. Make sure that you find out the answers to the following questions *before* you agree formally to a secondment:

✔ Is the secondment for a fixed term or for an indefinite period that may be subject to notice?

✔ Although your employer will generally be responsible for basic salary, what are the arrangements for overtime, bonuses, expenses, training etc?

✔ What will happen if long-term absence or persistent short-term absence occurs?

✔ How will supervisory and disciplinary matters be dealt with?

✔ If your secondment is long term, how will performance management and development be managed?

✔ Do you need to have indemnity insurance?

✔ Who will fill your usual role in your home organisation? How will you keep in touch?

Ways to set up a secondment yourself

Even if your employer doesn't have a seconding policy in place, it may be possible to persuade them to second you—if you can make a compelling case for the benefits. It might well be in the interests of a firm of solicitors, for example, to be perceived as altruistic or community-minded by allowing their staff to lend their skills to a deserving charity.

There are a number of organisations, many of them government sponsored, which specialise in seeking secondment opportunities for skilled workers. Below is just a selection (their website addresses are listed in the 'Useful links' section at the end of this chapter).

- **Business in the Community** has a membership of about 700 companies, and its purpose is 'to inspire, challenge, engage and support business in continually improving its positive impact on society'. The involvement of employees, supported and encouraged by their employers, is central to its work.
- **Employees in the Community Network** is for managers in any organisation that has an interest in employer-supported volunteering (including secondment), and aims to 'promote . . . employer-supported volunteering as a key part of company community involvement in the public, private, and voluntary sectors'. It offers various activities and services to promote this end, including network days and presentations on good practice.
- **Interchange** is a government initiative managed by the Cabinet Office which promotes and encourages the exchange of people and good practice between the civil service and other sectors of the economy. These include education, voluntary, health, public, private, and small business sectors.
- **The Whitehall and Industry Group** is an independent, membership organisation which brings senior people together to improve understanding and co-operation between the public, private, and voluntary sectors, and offers exchanges, leadership programmes, and events.

Step three: Check out the voluntary sector

There are many myths surrounding the voluntary sector: 'there are few paid jobs'; 'there's only limited scope for acquiring new skills'; 'working in the sector leads to a second class career', being just a few of them. None of these, however, is true. There are roughly 500,000 paid staff working in the sector (2.2 per cent of all UK employees, making it bigger than the electronics sector) along with three million unpaid volunteers. This means that there is scope for anyone, whatever their interests or skills, to find employment within it, whether paid or unpaid . . . particularly when you realise that around one in two organisations within the sector experience difficulties in recruiting staff!

Unsurprisingly then, the sector is extremely popular with career breakers, particularly given its other advantages:

✔ you gain an opportunity to undertake work in tune with your values

✔ you're rewarded by seeing the results of the work you do

✔ you escape from the 'rat-race'

✔ you usually work as part of a team of like-minded people

✔ you gain satisfaction from being able to contribute to an improvement in the fortunes of others

✔ regular employers are likely to look favourably on releasing you part time or for a set period to work for a 'good cause' and may well have a community relations budget for funding such schemes

✔ you have the chance to learn new skills in a completely different environment

Given the enormous scope of the voluntary sector, it's difficult to be specific here about what kinds of jobs are available or what the entry requirements are, as these are many and varied. However, the Voluntary Sector Skills website (listed at the end of the chapter) is a good place to begin the search for work that will suit you and your abilities.

Step four: Explore the options for travelling abroad

Not surprisingly, if you say the words 'career break' to most people, they immediately think of buying a round-the-world ticket or participating in projects in remote places. This is because travelling abroad does give you the perfect opportunity to do any of things we've already discussed above—expand your horizons, refresh your enthusiasm, learn a new skill, take a secondment, take part in voluntary work, and so on.

All kinds of organisations have been quick to spot this potential, and there are literally thousands of websites offering opportunities to work on conservation projects in Borneo, build orphanages in Uganda, teach in Romania, and many more.

Some of the best options might be to combine your various requirements. There is no comparison between taking an evening class in Italian in your local community centre and learning Italian in Pisa or Palermo, for example, or between studying Irish poetry at home and joining a course on Gaelic culture in Ireland. While holidaying in Costa Rica, you could also join a conservation project, or you could pre-empt your employer's team-building and leadership training courses by rafting on the Nile or leading a trek to Machu Picchu!

You may even find that combining a particular purpose with your desire to travel might give you an 'in' to certain countries that you wouldn't receive otherwise, or enable you to stay longer than you could simply as a tourist. For example, a student visa for Brazil to study Portuguese means you don't have to leave the country at regular intervals to renew. And in Japan, if you can obtain a cultural visa (granted to foreigners who find a sponsoring teacher to teach them some aspect of traditional Japanese culture), you are then permitted to work for up to 20 hours a week.

Travelling, and to an even greater degree, working in poorer communities, will give you a new outlook on life.

Comparatively, the people there have nothing material. Yet they have a much stronger sense of community and family, and living among the people will teach you to appreciate much more what we have in the more developed world.

TOP TIP
Many organisations that offer opportunities to work on overseas projects (such as Responsible Travel and GVI Expeditions listed below) are run in conjunction with governments, world agencies, and pioneering charities. Not only do you become deeply involved in the projects you're working on, but you may also be offered in-depth training.

Common mistakes

✗ You don't think big enough

A career break is an opportunity to do literally anything — whatever your particular dream might be. So why spend it doing something that you'd probably be able to do during the course of your normal life? It really is possible to go and climb Mount Kilimanjaro in aid of an African charity, or to help look after abandoned children in China. There are no limits, other than those you impose on yourself by not opening your mind!

✗ You don't think about the future

All good things come to an end, including career breaks. At some point or another you are going to need to come back to your regular life, and the more you have taken this into account when planning your break, the easier it will be. Make sure you know (and can explain clearly) what the benefits of your break might be to a potential employer. Alternatively, pin down the terms of your existing job with your current company; it's important that all parties involved in a secondment know where their responsibilities lie. Time spent ensuring that your break joins seamlessly with your future is best way to guarantee that it really is the best thing you've ever done.

STEPS TO SUCCESS

✔ Make sure your career break is properly planned, so that it becomes a life and career-enhancing experience, rather than simply a period of feeling at a loose end.

✔ Sort out your options with your employer. Will you be able to negotiate a paid sabbatical or unpaid study leave, or should you leave your job altogether?

✔ Would a secondment fulfil your need for new experience? If so, can you simply apply for one through your current job, or should you source your own opening?

✔ Check whether one of the myriad opportunities in the voluntary sector might suit your skills, interests, or experience. Could this be your chance to make a difference to your community, or someone else's, and do something worthwhile?

✔ Think global, and consider whether you could combine voluntary work or new learning with seeing the world, gaining new language skills, and experiencing different cultures.

Useful links

Business in the Community:
www.bitc.org.uk
Careerbreaker.com
www.careerbreaker.com
Employees in the Community Network:
www.volunteering.org.uk/workwith/eitcn.htm
Greenforce:
www.greenforce.org
Global Vision International:
www.gvi.co.uk
Interchange :
www.interchange.gov.uk
iVillage :
www.ivillage.co.uk
Learndirect:
www.learndirect.co.uk

National Council for Voluntary Organisations
www.ncvo-vol.org.uk
Responsible Travel:
www.responsibletravel.com
Voluntary Sector Skills:
www.voluntarysectorskills.org.uk
The Whitehall and Industry Group (WIG):
www.wig.co.uk

Sorting out your finances

4

Financing a career break can be an expensive business, and a as a result, money is the single consideration most likely to put people off taking a break.

There's a lot to think about. How will you pay for retraining or travel costs? How much do you need to save? What will you live on during your break? Are there any ways of bringing in extra income? Will you have to change your standard of living significantly? All these questions can build up into a major worry and prevent you from progressing any further, but with some careful forethought and self-discipline, financing can be really quite simple to manage.

Step one: Investigate what help there is around

In Chapter 3 we look at how employers might be prepared to continue paying you or to fund your new venture, depending on what type of break you take. There are many other kinds of financial help that you could explore instead or as well, though.

1 Grants

Many courses attract grants, depending either on the subject or your circumstances, and it's well worth finding out if you are eligible for one. The best place to start is with the Educational Grants Advisory Service (EGAS), which provides information and advice on all funding for post-16 education. This covers standard sources of funding such as grants, loans, bursaries and hardship funds, as well more unusual sources, such as educational trusts and charities.

The Service has a questionnaire you can fill in, and it will then check which funding might apply to you and send you the details. You can fill in this form online on the EGAS website (its address is listed below), and you can also get advice by calling their helpline on 020 7254 6251 (Monday, Wednesday, and Friday from 10am–12 noon and 2pm–4pm).

Alternatively, if you've already selected the course or training you want to do, it's worth contacting the college or training provider, or your local authority, to see what they can offer in the way of grants.

2 Loans

Loans are another option to think about. The most useful may be the Career Development Loan (CDL), which is a deferred repayment bank loan designed to help you pay for vocational learning or education. The Department for

Education and Skills (DfES) pays the interest on the loan while you're learning, and you then repay the loan to the bank over an agreed period at a fixed rate of interest. At the time of writing, CDLs are available through three high street banks: Barclays, The Co-operative Bank, and The Royal Bank of Scotland. You can borrow between £300 and £8,000 to fund up to two years of learning, plus (if relevant) up to one year's practical work experience where it forms part of the course.

For the full rules or a step-by-step guide to applying for a CDL, visit the Career Development Loans section on the Lifelong Learning website (address listed below), or call the CDL Information Line on 0800 585 505.

Other loan options

If you own your home, extending or increasing your mortgage could be one of the most cost-effective ways of financing your career break. Contact your mortgage provider to see if you can increase the amount of your loan, and how much the increase would cost you on a month-by-month basis. Alternatively you could think about transferring your mortgage to another lender with a better interest rate, and increasing the amount you borrow at the time of the transfer.

3 Allowances

Checking whether you are in line for unemployment benefit is another line of enquiry. You can't usually get the Jobseeker's

Allowance if you are on a full-time training programme, but you might be eligible if you are studying part time or doing an Open University course. You can find out more at your local Jobcentre or Social Security office, or via the Jobcentre Plus website (listed below).

TOP TIP
If you have chosen to study during your career break, remember that many courses— particularly online ones—are free. Others have means-tested fees, so you pay at a level you can afford. Use the Internet and check the small print in course specifications to see if you can cut your learning costs.

Step two: Explore ways of bringing in extra income

Whether or not you receive a loan or grant, extra income when you're not earning your usual salary is always useful. Thinking creatively may help you find all sorts of ways of bringing in money; here are just a few suggestions to start you off.

1 Use your house
If you are planning to leave your home for an extended period, you have four options: to leave the property unoccupied; ask a friend or contact to house-sit; find

a tenant either independently or through a letting agency, or register with a house-swapping agency. Either of the last two would seem the most sensible, as they both enable you to use the empty house to generate income!

✔ Letting

Once they've overcome any discomfort at the idea of strangers living in their house, thousands of people each year are delighted to discover how easy this is. An agency will screen applicants, collect rent, and deal with problems in your absence—all for a fee of around 10 per cent of the rent. If you want to maximise the income, you can always organise the rental yourself, normally through advertising in your local newspaper, magazine, or website read by the kind of people you want as tenants.

✔ House swapping

You can also consider swapping your home (and sometimes your car too) with a family in the city or country that you want to visit. Exchanging houses not only saves accommodation costs, it immediately takes you off the tourist trail and sets you down where 'real people' live. The two main requirements are that you be willing to spend at least a few weeks in one place, and that you have a decent house in a potentially desirable location. Most swaps are arranged six months or more in advance for up to a month at a time (usually in the summer), and an Internet search will supply details of thousands of home exchange agencies who can match up compatible swappers. The great advantage of a home swap is that this is not a commercial transaction, so the costs are relatively low.

TOP TIP
Always ask prospective tenants to supply references from their current employer, bank, and previous landlord.

---

2 Get some sponsorship

Writing to targeted companies asking for sponsorship; holding pub quizzes, raffles and auctions; throwing themed parties; holding cake sales or selling off surplus possessions at car boot sales; running marathons, or organising sponsored swims . . . all these and many, many others are tried and tested ways of raising money from your local community, friends and families. Almost anything you can think of goes, in terms of sponsorship — as long as you bear two important points in mind:

- it's much easier to raise £3,000 in small donations from lots of people than to persuade one organisation or individual to part with the whole amount. More is more, in this instance, so make sure you have plenty of different ideas—especially if you're trying to reach a particular target.
- you need to include the cost of what you are doing in the amount you need to raise. There's no point in spending £100 on baked beans with which to fill a bath, if you're only going to raise £90 by sitting in it!

3 Take on a part-time job

As millions of students will testify, taking on casual or part-time work can be an invaluable way of financing the activities that you really want to concentrate on. Try investigating your local supermarkets for night-shift work, or see whether pubs in your area need extra bar staff. In these days of '24/7', there are always work opportunities during the odder or smaller hours, leaving you free to pursue your career break dream for the rest of the time.

Step three: Streamline your finances

As the plethora of Alvin Hall-type financial gurus on TV would suggest, *all* of us in western societies could live more efficiently and cheaply if we made the effort. Well the moment has arrived . . . during your career break, you *need* to make the effort. Only you can know the details of what your commitments are and where your money goes, but there are many simple steps that everyone can take. And it's amazing what an enormous difference they can make to the level of your outgoings.

✔ **Renegotiate your repayment levels.** Do you have the cheapest mortgage rate available on the market? What about your house/car/life insurance? Credit card rate? And your utility suppliers—do you use them simply because you always have done, or because they offer best value for money? Most of us are too lazy or too uninterested even to think about what we spend on essential bills, but it's highly likely that you could save thousands a year simply by investigating alternative suppliers. Money Supermarket (link below) is a great place to start shopping around for better deals.

✔ **Restructure your debts.** If you have outstanding debts, particularly on store cards or other expensive loan schemes, it's important to get them under control. For example, if you have several credit cards all demanding hefty payments every month, it may be better to consolidate them into one personal loan, allowing you to restructure your monthly repayments at a level you can afford. The interest charged will depend on the amount you need to borrow—and beware of early redemption penalties (often equivalent to two months' payments). Again, many websites such as Money Supermarket are good places to find the best rates on personal loans. If you have happen to have any sort of real problem with debt, the Consumer Credit Counselling Service helps to negotiate repayment plans that suit both lenders and borrowers, and can be contacted on 0800 138 1111.

✔ **'Mothball' your non-urgent commitments.** Yes, your baby's university fund *is* important. But he's only 18 months old at the moment, and it won't be disastrous if you take a six-month holiday from paying into it (as long as you remember to restart the payments when you're earning again). Are there any other expenses or outgoings that you can defer for a while?

TOP TIP
**Many mortgage and other lenders and offer
'payment holidays' as part of their agreement
with you. Would it be helpful to defer some
of your larger outgoings during your
career break until you are back at work?
Remember that this will only help if you
make CERTAIN that you restart the
payments once you are earning again.**

Step four: Live within your new means

Working out a budget is an easy thing to do. You add up all your essential outgoings—food, accommodation, transport, bills, and so on, and come up with the minimum amount of money that you need to live on. However, then comes the hard bit . . . sticking to it!

While you're living on reduced means, you simply have to face the fact that you need to be disciplined. One excellent way of helping yourself to do this is, every time you're tempted to spend money you shouldn't, work out what you *won't* be able to do as a consequence.

For example, say you are spending your career break travelling round the world. If you crack and spend £50 on a pair of jeans, that's a day rafting on the Zambezi that you've missed! Looked at this way, it's much easier to forego your 'essential' monthly facial, or to resist the 'bargain' Playstation.

Step five: Protect your financial future

It's very easy to get so carried away by the excitement of planning a career break that you take your eye off possible consequences for the future. Do tread warily, though, and make sure you don't jeopardise your long-term financial wellbeing—or at least, not without consciously deciding to do so. Below are just two of the pitfalls that you might encounter:

■ depending on which industry sector you work in, **a career break can severely affect your pension and/or conditions of service**. This is particularly true of the public sector (teaching and the health service, for example), especially since more and more institutions have been self-governing. Be careful that your break does not affect your continuous service record, for instance, or benefits such as sick pay entitlement could suffer significantly.

■ **failing to maintain your National Insurance contributions can also have adverse effects** on your entitlement to future government grants and benefits. While there are various exemptions from having to pay National Insurance depending on how you are spending your career break, it is still advisable to check out your situation with the Inland Revenue. For example, although you may be exempt from Class 1 contributions (payable on your regular salary), you may be wise to choose to pay Class 3 contributions (a voluntary means of protecting your right to contributory benefits) instead. Your local IR office will be able to help you choose the right course for your individual circumstances.

Although you may not be affected by either of these situations, the point is that you *must* make sure you know what you're doing and don't get caught unawares.

Common mistakes

✗ You carry on blithely as you've always done
The fastest way to spoil the beneficial effects of a career break is to come back to discover that you've run up large debts or defaulted on essential payments during your absence! It's *vital* that you think through your circumstances and make the necessary plans and arrangements before embarking on your break so that you can move back smoothly into your regular life at the end of it.

✗ You fail to lay sufficient contingency plans
You may well have catered for the costs of your career break itself, but have you remembered to set anything aside in case of unexpected events? What will happen if you or one of your dependants falls ill or has an accident, for example? Have you thought about how you'd meet an increase in mortgage rates? It's a very good idea

always to keep the equivalent of three months' salary stashed away somewhere safe, *just in case*. That way, you'll always have peace of mind and be able to enjoy your new experience without the lurking fear that you're flying too close to the wind.

STEPS TO SUCCESS

✔ Check out what financial help may be available to you, whether it's in the form of continuous pay from your employer, grants, loans, or allowances that you may be entitled to.

✔ Consider possible ways of boosting your income or raising funds, from getting yourself sponsored to letting out your house.

✔ Streamline your cost of living by re-negotiating essential costs such as mortgage payments; switch to cheaper suppliers of everything possible, from utilities to insurance; 'mothball' any non-urgent commitments until after your break, and consolidate your debts.

✔ Analyse your financial requirements honestly, then set yourself a budget and live within it.

✔ Protect your financial future by ensuring that your break doesn't jeopardise employee benefits or pensions, and keeping up your National Insurance payments.

Useful links

Department for Education and Skills:
www.dfes.gov.uk/index.shtml
The Educational Grants Advisory Service (EGAS):
www.egas-online.org.uk
Inland Revenue:
www.inlandrevenue.gov.uk
Jobcentre Plus:
www.jobcentreplus.gov.uk
Lifelong learning:
www.lifelonglearning.co.uk/cdl
Money matters to me:
www.moneymatterstome.co.uk
Money Supermarket:
www.moneysupermarket.com

Investigating flexible working

In Chapter 1, we outlined some alternative routes to taking some time away from the office if your request for a career break is turned down. Working flexibly is an increasingly popular option for many people today, and this chapter offers advice on how to see if it's an arrangement that might work for you. The important thing is to find out if this is a route open to you. If it is, you can then move on to make a persuasive case!

Step one: Find out how to apply

✔ First of all, make sure that you qualify for flexible working arrangements. Most people apply for flexible working because of their family situation. As of April 2003 and under the terms of the Employment Act 2002, parents of children under the age of 6, or of less abled-bodied children under the age of 18 may request flexible working hours, but they need to have completed six months' continuous service at the company or organisation in question before making that request. Some organisations may also consider flexible working if you need to care for a dependent adult, such as your spouse, partner, or parent.

✔ Check the employees' handbook or with your human

resources department (if you have one) to see what the preferred method of application is. The DTI has some basic forms that may be customised, so your company may be using these already. If not, most companies would expect a request for a change in working hours to be made in writing. This should be followed up within 28 days by a meeting between you and your manager. Bear in mind that only one application can be made in any 12-month period.

✔ Do some informal research. Once you've checked out your company's policy, speak to friends or colleagues who have applied for flexible working hours or who already are working under a new arrangement. How did the successful applicants approach their request? Are they finding it easier or harder than they'd anticipated to work in a new way? Bear in mind that if your working arrangements are changed, these changes are permanent unless otherwise agreed between you and your employer.

Step two: Make a persuasive case

✔ Prepare your case and try to anticipate the questions your manager may ask you when you meet to talk about your application. Requests can be turned down because managers fear that flexible working arrangements may affect the business, so be prepared to give well thought-out, positive responses to questions such as:

- Will you still be able be an effective team member?
- How would a change in your working hours affect your colleagues?
- What will be the overall effect on the work you do?
- How could a change in your working hours affect the business positively?

TOP TIP
Be realistic and also be ready to compromise. A popular way of approaching negotiations of any type is to draw up a wish-list for your successful outcome that contains an ideal solution, a realistic one, and an absolute minimum. If you show that *you* are prepared to be flexible, your manager is more likely to be flexible too.

✔ Think about when you would want any new arrangement to start and give your company as much notice as you can. This will convey the fact that you are still committed to the company and are thinking about how the potential changes to your working life will fit in overall.

✔ Stress that the quality of your work and your motivation will not change, even if your working hours do. In fact, you'll be more productive as you'll suffer from less stress and will need to take fewer days off sick to look after your children or dependants when they are ill. You could also explain that as part of a reciprocal arrangement whereby all parties benefit, you'd be willing to work extra or longer in times of heavy demand.

Finally, but no less importantly, explain how much knowledge and expertise you have built up while you have been working there and how much the company benefits from it.

TOP TIP

Many companies or organisations will allow you to bring a union representative with you to a meeting to discuss your application. If you do invite one along, make sure he or she has read a copy of your application and any related documents from your place of work so that he or she is up to speed.

Step three: Follow up

According to the DTI guidelines, you should be informed about the outcome of your application within 14 days of your meeting.

✔ If all goes well and an agreement is reached, your new working arrangement and an agreed start date should be set down in writing and copies given to all relevant parties (you, your manager, and the HR department or representative if you have one).

✔ If your request is not granted, you may appeal within 14 days of receiving the decision. See the DTI website (www.dti.gov.uk) for further advice on this issue.

Common mistakes

✗ You don't prepare your case properly

However confident you feel about your application for flexible working, it's a really good idea to write down some notes or prompts to take into any meetings you have about it. They'll be very useful if you get flustered or forget any of your key points. Spend as much time as you can thinking through potential questions that your boss may ask you, and be sure you can get across clearly how your career break would benefit the business.

✗ You're inflexible

Remember that, even if you e-mailed your boss about your plans before you met with him or her, they may still be reeling from the fact that they may be losing a valuable member of staff for a good stretch of time. While it's important to be sure of your rights, it's also important not to damage your relationship with your boss and colleagues: at the very least, you'll need a good reference before you leave, and if you'd like your job to be kept open for you until you're back, you can't really manage without them! Be assertive but polite and try to see the process as another type of business negotiation.

STEPS TO SUCCESS

✓ If you're not sure whether you're eligible to apply for flexible working, ask someone from your company's

HR department (if there is one), or visit the DTI website. There may also be helpful information in your company's staff handbook.

✔ Ask friends and colleagues who have been through the same process if they can offer any advice. Is there anything they would do differently this time?

✔ As you get ready to talk to your boss about your plans, prepare your case well and try to anticipate questions you might be asked.

✔ Be ready to compromise—you can't have everything all your own way—and remember that if you're reasonable, your boss is more likely to try and meet you half-way.

Useful links

Acas A to Z of Work:
www.acas.org.uk/a_z/working_parents.html
Business Link:
www.businesslink.gov.uk/bdotg/action/home
Department of Trade and Industry Employment Relations:
www.dti.gov.uk/er/flexible.htm
iVillage.co.uk:
**www.ivillage.co.uk/workcareer/worklife/archive/
0,,202,00.html**
Working Families:
**www.workingfamilies.org.uk/asp/home_zone/
m_welcome.asp**

Getting back into the swing of things

As mentioned back in Chapter 1, people take career breaks for many reasons: to look after family members, to start a family, for self-development, to satisfy an interest in other cultures, to recover from illness, to complete personal projects, or to recharge their batteries following redundancy. Whatever your reasons for stopping, there comes a moment when your attention turns back to the world of work.

You may have an agreement to return to the same employer after your break, you may be looking for pastures new, or your financial circumstances may have changed. Whatever the reason, being clear about what you want and what you have to offer employers will move you closer to achieving your goals. Take some time to consider your career plan and your objectives for returning. For example:

- What is the core purpose of work for you and what else do you hope to get from working?
- How much of this do you expect to achieve immediately and how much within three years?

Think over all of these issues and then review your strengths. What knowledge, skills,

achievements, facets of your personality, and potential would you like to use at work?

Step one: Lay your worries to rest

1 Will my previous experience count, even after several years away?

Many people returning to work after a break worry that their skills and knowledge will be out of date and therefore won't count. As we discussed on p 3, if it's a while since you worked or if you need a registration to practise, you may need to refresh your skills. The key thing to bear in mind, though, is that previous experience *does* count: it tells your employer that you are capable of success in the role that you did previously. It's also reassuring to you that you'll be able to perform in the future, since you were successful before.

2 Will my self-confidence return?

Confidence in your ability to do a good job can drop when you've been away from your work for a while. This is particularly the case after illness, redundancy, or a maternity break, and returners often doubt their ability to cope with their busy and responsible job. Don't worry! Lots of people take up the challenge every year and are successful, enjoying their return to the office and even returning to more high-profile jobs. Making sure you are up-to-date with all the latest policies, technologies, and skills will help you break back into the working world more easily. The best recipe for building confidence is getting out there and proving to yourself step-by-step that you can do it.

Step two: Plan the return to your old job

If you're planning to return to the same job, it's a good plan to keep up some regular contact with your team to reassure them of your ongoing commitment and enthusiasm and to keep yourself informed about changes. Step up this contact in the two weeks before you return and make sure that you widen this activity to all your regular working contacts.

TOP TIP

Be sensitive in the way that you interact with your boss, colleagues, and staff. Some of them may have carried an extra workload in your absence and deserve your appreciation. Some may feel threatened by your return; others may be reluctant to give up tasks and responsibilities they have enjoyed while you've been away. Be tactful and do your best to keep open good channels of communication between you.

You may also have home-based issues to think about as you prepare to return to work. If you have children or relatives to look after, you'll need to make sure they're settled into childcare or alternative caring arrangements for the times

---

that you're out of the house. If you have a partner to share these commitments with, talk over the various options available to you so that you work out an arrangement that's workable for you both. Whether you have a partner or not, you could always club together with other parents or carers to make options more affordable or convenient.

Returning to work after redundancy

If your job has been made redundant, try not to let it demoralise you. You're bound to feel low at times, but taking some positive action will help you get back on track. Firstly, think about the market you have been working in. Is it expanding or shrinking? Your answer to this will help you decide whether to return to the same sector or try your luck elsewhere. Think about your strengths and skills and how you could transfer these to other roles. If you're not sure of current trends, ask people you know to give you a steer. Talk to your former boss and colleagues if you have a good relationship with them and ask if they have any recommendations about who you should be talking to as part of your job search. This will help keep your networks growing.

It's extremely important to keep in touch with people and even to expand your networks if you can. Many job vacancies are 'hidden', in that they're not advertised widely, so you never know when talking to the right person at the right time might put you on to a lead that proves perfect for you.

Prepare a positive statement to use if you are asked during an interview why you were made redundant. Ideally, this should be a very short description of the contraction in the market or the restructuring of your department or organisation, followed by a forward-looking statement about the skills you hope to build on and where you want to go with your career. Also prepare a description of how you spent your time away from work, how it benefited you, and how the experience will add value to your next employer's business.

Step three: Look for a new role

Sometimes, you might not want to return to your old job, or you may not be able to for a variety of reasons. It's time, then, to look for a new role to challenge you.

A gap on a chronological CV is bound to be noticed by prospective employers and will probably get a knee-jerk adverse reaction, so make sure that you highlight what you've been doing with your time in positive terms. If, after a while, you find you are still getting negative reactions, try writing a 'skills-based' or 'functional' CV. This type of CV focuses attention on your strengths and achievements; an employer decides whether they're interested in the first few seconds of reading, well before noticing your career break on the second page.

Whichever type of CV you write, you need to get across the *benefits* your career break has brought whenever the question arises with prospective employers. Perhaps you have demonstrated initiative, patience, people skills, planning and organising, or confidence and determination. Highlight any new skills, even if you don't feel that they are relevant to the posts you are applying for, as they demonstrate your ability to learn.

TOP TIP

Jobhunting can be tiring and deflating at times, so it's important to keep yourself feeling up-beat. Do this by making a little progress on your jobsearch every day. Make sure that you make the most of *all* the routes to market: replying to advertisements, posting your CV on Internet job sites, registering with agencies, approaching companies direct, and networking with people you know.

Chapter 7 offers plenty of useful advice if you are thinking of making a change in career direction.

Step four: Make the most of the honeymoon period in a new job

Congratulations, you've got the job! You may have a formal induction to give you a basic grounding in the information you need, but it's still sensible to think about how you can make a good initial impression. In the first week, get to grips with exactly what your objectives are. Clarity is the watchword here. In some roles you'll be expected to make an impact very early, while in other roles there may be a longer honeymoon period. You need to know what's expected of you when, and how your objectives fit into those of the team and the organisation. Getting to know specifics about people, like a department head's agenda or a key client's pet hates, will help you to navigate the potential pitfalls and find the easy routes to achieving your goals. Putting all the information together will allow you to understand how and why the organisation functions best.

The second week is best spent finding out more about who's who and creating the communication channels you'll need to get your job done. Meet with as many key people as you can, as this will help you to handle any political aspects of your role well. During the third week you can begin to develop a clear picture of how to best play things in your own terms. Ask yourself:

- What am I going to be doing?
- How am I going to achieve it?
- What do people in this business need to know about me, my skills, and past achievements?
- How am I going to get that message out?

Start a role fresh, in two senses:

- Put behind you the worries that you had in your previous

role. For example, if you had a difficult relationship with your boss in your last position, lay that to rest and don't dwell on it. Don't carry old insecurities into your next job—things are different now. Visualise how you want things to be and start on the first day as if they were already so.

■ Be well rested, but prepared to go home feeling exhausted. If you're not taking on information like a sponge in the early weeks, then something odd is going on. Plan a very quiet first weekend or two so that you can rest, digest the information, and make sense of what you've learnt.

Common mistakes

✗ You suffer from culture shock

Humans find change stressful, and even changes that we want and actively seek out have an effect on our minds and bodies. Recognise that you may experience culture shock initially when you return to work and decide in advance how you can help yourself cope. Accentuate the positive when chatting with people at work, both about your time away and about your return. Your colleagues may feel that you are lucky to have had a break (those without children may not appreciate what hard work having a new baby is!) and may resent what they see as 'whinging' about the difficulties of returning. On the other hand, it's important not to bottle up any negative feelings—not everyone can slot back in to their old life straightaway. Find an appropriate and sympathetic friend, coach, or mentor to share your thoughts with and to support you during this time.

✗ You want to be the conquering hero or heroine

Some people expect to be greeted with awe and fascination by their team when they return to their old job and are surprised to be facing a very negative atmosphere, one sometimes made up of jealousy, hostility, defensiveness, and for managers, loss of authority. Try to react with understanding to your colleagues and don't expect too much attention. Throw yourself into your work and have confidence that your performance and your personality will soon bring people around. Be patient and remember that an atmosphere of this sort rarely lasts if you remain positive.

✗ You don't 'sell' the benefits of your break

Unless you spread the word yourself, people may not recognise what a break has done for you. It may not be clear what additional skills you now have and how these can benefit your team and organisation. Whether you're chatting with colleagues or being grilled at interview by a panel of managers, it pays to have done your homework and to have really thought about what you have gained and how you can persuade others of the benefits. If you raised an amount of money for charity and developed your organisational and influencing skills in the process, say so and be proud of it.

STEPS TO SUCCESS

✔ Remember that your previous experience does count, even if you need to refresh your knowledge of your existing skills or gain new ones. You have been a successful worker in the past, and there's no reason why you can't be one in the future.

✔ Try not to worry about your abilities too much; your confidence will grow as you get back into the swing of things.

✔ If you plan to return to your old job, keep in regular touch with your team during your time away and increase this contact as your start-date gets nearer.

✔ Remember that it will take people a little while to get used to you being back, just as it will take you time to be comfortable again back in your old setting. Try not to expect too much too soon.

✔ Try not to step on anyone's toes, especially those who have been covering for you in your absence; they may have enjoyed the extra responsibility or different tasks they've been doing while you've been away, and may be reluctant to give them up.

✔ Being made redundant can be a very demoralising experience. Try to keep upbeat by taking some positive action, though. Explore your options and work out if this is in fact a time for you to spread your wings and try a completely new field of work. Keep in touch with people who can help you: many job vacancies are 'hidden' and not widely advertised, and your network is a good way of finding out about them.

✔ Don't feel that you have to explain in great depth why you have been made redundant. Many redundancies are a result of external forces, such as changes in a market or a larger company reorganisation, none of which reflects on you. Summarise briefly what happened then move on to state positively what you are looking for in your next job move.

✔ Always be positive and enthusiastic about your career break. Emphasise what you've learned and what you've achieved.

✔ If you decide to look for a new job, think about the type of CV you want to use. A standard, chronological CV will show up a career break clearly. If you want to downplay your break or move into a new field, you might want to use a function or skills-based CV instead, as this will emphasise your talents and strengths more than your previous career history.

✔ Once you're in your new job, your main priority is to find exactly what's expected of you and when. Try and meet the people you'll be dealing with most frequently in your second week so that you can work out how best to take your relationship forward.

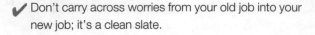 Don't carry across worries from your old job into your new job; it's a clean slate.

Useful links

CIPD.co.uk:
www.cipd.co.uk/mandq/develop/cpd/careerbreaks.htm
Totaljobs.com:
www.totaljobs.com
Women Returners' Network:
www.women-returners.co.uk

Looking for a new challenge

When jobs were for life, you decided what line of work you wanted, worked hard, and the career path was pretty much mapped out for you. The working world has changed. If you've just come back from a career break and have decided not to go back to your old job, the good news is that career paths are more flexible—your experiences on your time out may really help you get back on (or further up!) your chosen career ladder. You can now choose a spiral path, stepping through different fields or functions: many employers encourage the growth in ideas that a diverse workforce offers, and they also value the different perspectives offered by those from outside their industry.

As career breaks are more common today, even transitory career paths are possible. These are popular with people who like variety, novelty, or have other worthwhile priorities. If you require periods of employment interspersed with breaks that will give you time to study, travel, raise a family, start a business, or care for elderly or unwell family members, this option could be for you.

There are, however, still expert career paths for those who want to specialise in a particular field and traditional, 'linear' careers for those who enjoy the challenge, responsibility, and status of climbing the hierarchical ladder. Whatever your set of circumstances, it's a good idea to create a career plan and to ask yourself: what does your career need to do for *you*?

Step one: Start your research

1 What's the difference between a career plan and a development plan?

Your career plan maps out long-term objectives, your more immediate objectives, and how you want your life and work to fit together. Your development plan maps out the skills and experience gaps for the different steps along the way and how you will address those. In effect, the development plan enables the career plan to work.

2 How do I find out what jobs I might be suitable for?

If you are naturally curious and chatty, you could start your research by talking to people. Make use of your contacts and ask for names and contact details of people who might be able to help with each of the options you're considering. This approach not only increases your network but it also gets you the targeted information you need. It may also put you in touch with contacts who can quite often open doors for you.

On the other hand, you may prefer to get started with some Internet or library research and save the networking until you feel a little better informed about possibilities. Neither approach is right or wrong, but people who use *both* approaches are likely to be the best prepared, most knowledgeable, and 'luckiest' when it comes to opportunities.

3 Will frequent job moves look bad on my CV?

It depends on what is 'normal' for your market. In IT, for example, regular moves are common. A CV that shows frequent moves is less likely to be frowned on if the skills offered and achievements shown are relevant to the job you're applying for now. If it is clear that in each role you've occupied you've been promoted or selected for specific strengths or skills, then employers will see you as a sought-after individual rather than a job hopper.

Step two: Be self-aware

Now that you're back from your travels, it's a good time to review your career so far, asking yourself some key questions. These will help you work out the best next step for you. For example:

■ what expertise do you have?

- what achievements are you proud of?
- what work have you received praise and recognition for?
- what were the outcomes of these achievements for your clients, team, or organisation? what flair or talents have you not yet fully used?
- do you have areas of untapped potential?

Also think about the skills you've used throughout your career so far and any differences in the way you've worked from job to job.

✔ Go through a typical working week writing down each skill, strength, or knowledge area that you have used on a separate piece of paper or Post-it note. Do this for each job you've held.

✔ Next, cluster your notes, grouping those that fit together and giving each group a title, such as 'Organising', 'Communicating', or 'People skills'. Doing this will identify and organise your transferable skills and help you be clearer about what you're offering other employers.

✔ Finally, draw other elements into the mix. As yourself:

- what does my career need to do for me (and my family)?
- what do I value in work?
- what makes a job satisfying?
- what would I or do I hate in a job?

TOP TIP

It's well worth taking some time to think about these questions, and to be honest with yourself as you do it. They'll help you work out what you want to achieve and what might be holding you back, such as financial obligations or geographical preferences.

Step three: Do a market and trend analysis

If you're keen to stay in the market you're currently in, think about the way it seems to be moving—it may have changed while you were away on your break.

- What do you like about the market you're currently in?
- What are the trends within this function and industry?
- How might these affect your prospects going forwards?

Think in broad terms about who might have a need for your skills. What goals or problems could you help them with and what else can you offer them?

These are big and wide-ranging questions, so to help you focus on them, do some research.

✔ Use the Internet and your network of friends and colleagues to expand your knowledge of companies and organisations, and of their internal trends and needs.

✔ Read all you can in journals and newspapers about the markets you are most interested in and identify relevant professional bodies for information on trends and the market for relevant skills. Libraries and Chambers of Commerce can be good sources of local information.

TOP TIP
The more questions you ask, the more you'll know about what direction you want to go forward in. Research often gets easier as you go along, so don't be put off too early!

Step four: Match up your planning with your goals

To get the best from your research and planning, you need to have a clear goal or set of goals ahead. The '3–1–6–1' approach mentioned in Chapter 2 is very helpful here too.

✔ Ask yourself what you'd like your life to be like in three years' time and write down what comes to mind in as much detail as you can.

✔ Write in the present tense, as if it has already happened.

✔ Repeat this for one year's time, six months' time and one month's time. Your plan should give you clarity and motivation for the long-term future. It breaks down the bigger picture of your life into an actionable plan that you can start on right now.

A 'reality check' will help you recognise the right opportunity when it arises. Spend time on this when you are job hunting.

✔ Divide a page into four quadrants, headed 'Role', 'Organisation', 'Package', and 'Boss'.

✔ Now ask yourself what you want from your next career move.

✔ Think about the 'ingredients' that make up your ideal role, putting these into the quadrants on your page.

Once your criteria are mapped out in this way, you'll have visual aid that will help you to weigh up the opportunities that come your way. When you're invited to interview for a new job, you can use the sheet to come up with strong, targeted questions about the potential role and the organisation.

Step five: Develop yourself

You've now identified your own skills and your immediate and longer-term goals. Is there a direct match already or will employers see gaps? If there are, identify what those gaps are and prioritise them, working out what you need to learn. Divide each gap down into bite-sized 'chunks' of learning or experience required.

TOP TIP
Think about you learn best. Do you prefer to
read books, listen to an expert, try things out

**yourself, or practice with supervision?
Knowing your preferred learning
style, and sticking to it, will help
you really make things happen,
rather than put them off.**

Step six: Market yourself

Marketing yourself may sound like a strange concept, but it's an important part of career planning. It's particularly important if you've been out of the loop for a while, as you'll need to spread the word about what you can do and why you'd be a great employee.

Let's look at three examples of how self-marketing works and how it might fit into your objectives.

- During the **honeymoon period in a new job**, your objective is to establish good communication channels with your new colleagues and contacts and build a practical network. Here, then, marketing yourself will focus on attracting the interest of people who will make your work easier.
- Once you feel **established in your new role**, your objective is to make sure that interesting work is offered to you, so self-marketing in *this* context will focus more on bringing your successes and achievements to light.
- When **looking for new roles**, your objective is to attract offers that meet your criteria. Your self-marketing

now will focus on getting yourself noticed by the right employers.

As we can see, self-marketing is continuous but it will change in nature depending on where you are in your career and what your ideal next step is. Whatever you're doing, though, think about your 'audience' and what is important to them. You may be offering to solve problems, deliver a product or service, improve quality, or develop something new. To grab and maintain their attention, you need to focus on the outcomes of your activities as they're relevant to your audience: for example, these could be increased profits, customer satisfaction and retention, or improvements in efficiency.

Common mistakes

✗ **You have unrealistic ambitions**
If you don't take the time to look at your industry's trends and their impact on your market, you'll end up with a career plan that's completely unrealistic. The wealth of information on the Internet in particular means that there's little excuse for remaining ignorant about issues that may affect your future success. Even if you're not online at home, you can use an Internet café or just visit your local library to find out what you need to know. Make it your business to be informed and don't be afraid to ask 'difficult' questions of people in the know— experts love the opportunity to shine and will be flattered that you've asked them.

✗ You don't do anything

A plan works by acting as a catalyst for specific and related actions which together create the desired effect. There's absolutely no point in writing a plan, carrying out the first action, and then leaving it to gather dust. You have to be ready to keep plugging away at your to-do list in order to get a good result. You may get downhearted at times—you're only human—but try to keep setbacks in perspective and to keep your goal in sight.

STEPS TO SUCCESS

✔ A career plan is useful whatever your career stage, but it can be of particular help when you've just come back from a career break and are thinking about the options open to you.

✔ Sometimes, it's useful to look back before you start to look forward. As a first step, review the shape of your career so far: are you happy with the way things are (or have been) or do you want to change it in someway?

✔ Be honest with yourself as you think about the past, present, and future.

✔ Whether you're keen to stay in an industry you have experience of or you want a change of scene, look at that industry's current trends so that you can see how your skills would fit in. What can you offer that would make you stand out from the crowd?

✔ To make sure that you're clear about your goals (and as a result, that you can put your research and planning to the best use), do a '3–1–6–1' plan. It will break down the 'bigger picture' into smaller action points that you can start to work on.

✔ If you need to develop new skills to update your existing talents or to gain a completely new string to your bow, do something about it!

✔ Keep your motivation up. If you feel put off by what lies ahead rather than energised, look again at your schedule. It's probably too tight, so readjust it to something more sensible.

✔ Make some noise and market yourself! Even if you have fantastic skills and are a dream to work with, no-one will know unless you tell them. This doesn't mean you have to be pushy or arrogant, but that you tailor what you do to what your 'audience' requires.

Useful links

British Chambers of Commerce:
www.britishchambers.org.uk
The Open University's Careers Advisory Service:
www.open.ac.uk/learners-guide/careers
Totaljobs.com:
www.totaljobs.com/editorial/getadvice/index.shtm

Where to find more help

Be Your Own Life Coach: How to Take Control of Your Life and Achieve Your Wildest Dreams
Fiona Harrold
London: Coronet Books, 2001
256pp ISBN: 0340770643
If you're thinking about taking a career break, you may feel already that you're at a crossroads in your life. If you're not sure which direction to take next, this book will help you take stock of your current position and think about next steps. This best-selling book is full of inspiring and practical advice on how to change your life and reach your goals.

Gap Years for Grown Ups
Susan Griffith
Oxford: Vacation Work Publications
256pp ISBN: 1854583182
If you didn't have a gap year the first time round, you may be feeling a yearning to take some time out and travel. If so, this book is full of information on different ways to spend your time abroad, from joining a specialist programme to taking on voluntary work or simply taking in the sights. The book also contains case histories from people who have taken the plunge a little later in life.

The Money Diet
Martin Lewis
London: Vermilion, 2004
372pp ISBN: 0091894840
If cash is tight and you're trying to save up to fund a career break, this easy-to-read book is a very helpful place to start. The author is a financial journalist and he claims to be able to save the average family up to £6,000 per year, all of which would help towards funding your time away. Billing itself 'the ultimate smart consumers' guide', *The Money Diet* also has a website you can visit to find out more.